C&RT

The Creatrix Inventory

Richard E. Byrd

Amsterdam • Johannesburg • Oxford
San Diego • Sydney • Toronto

Part I. Identifying Tendencies

The Creatrix Inventory is designed to help members of an organization explore some characteristics that can affect the way they contribute to the success of that organization. Specifically, it will help you determine to what degree you possess these characteristics.

INSTRUCTIONS

Read each item of the Creatrix Inventory and respond by writing a number from one to nine in the space provided. A "9" indicates complete agreement with the statement, a "1" indicates complete disagreement, a "5" indicates moderate agreement (or moderate disagreement), and the other numbers should be used to indicate varying degrees of agreement.

The spaces for your responses alternate from the left side to the right side of the statements. When you complete the inventory, the numbers in the left blanks should be totaled and then the numbers in the right blanks should be totaled. You will score your own inventory. Because an accurate assessment is important, be as honest as possible with your responses. There are no "right" or "wrong" answers, so avoid responding in terms of how you think a person *should* respond. Each category that results from this inventory contains both strengths and weaknesses, so trying to beat the system will not make a person look "better"; it could, however, produce an *inaccurate* picture of the person.

There is no time limit, but you should not debate long over any item.

The Creatrix Inventory

9 = **Complete agreement**   1 = **Complete disagreement**

_8_ I can put off until tomorrow what I ought to do today.

Daydreaming is a useful activity. _6_

_5_ I determine my own moral values.

I often have sexual fantasies. _8 6_

_4_ I feel free not to do what others expect of me.

Being creative is the greatest human attribute. _4_

_7_ I accept my weaknesses.

I like new ways better than tried and true ways. _5_

_7_ I generally expect success.

There are a variety of solutions to every problem. _6_

_4_ It is possible for me to live the way I want to.

Ideas are more important than people are. _2_

(Do not compute totals or subtotals until you finish the inventory.)

_35_ **Subtotal for Left Column**   **Subtotal for Right Column** _34 29_

35
/46
Left Subtotal Brought Forward   **Right Subtotal Brought Forward** 3̶1̶ 29
39

9 I can cope with the ups and downs of life.

People are more dissimilar than alike. 3

6 In dealing with others, I believe in saying what I feel.

I believe "Nothing ventured, nothing gained." 7

6 I can "stick my neck out" in my relations with others.

I often see a humorous side when others do not. 9

4 I live in terms of my wants, likes, dislikes, and values.

My ideas are usually better than the ideas of others. 5

8 I trust my ability to size up a situation.

Restrictions are for the average person. 1

7 I have an innate capacity to cope with life.

I am an above-average person. 6

4 I can feel right without always having to please others.

What others consider chaos does not bother me. 5

2 I will risk a friendship in order to say or do what I believe is right.

Complete ambiguity is more desirable than complete clarity. 3

(Do not compute totals or subtotals until you finish the inventory.)

81 **Subtotal for Left Column**   **Subtotal for Right Column** 68

_81_ **Left Subtotal Brought Forward   Right Subtotal Brought Forward** _68_

43   31

_4_   I feel free to be myself whatever the consequences.

I pay little attention to time.   _4_

_6_   I feel free to show both friendly and unfriendly feelings to strangers.

Inventors contribute more than political leaders do.   _8_

_4_   I enjoy detachment and privacy.

My childhood was lonely.   _1_

_7_   I am assertive and positive.

I sometimes think I am crazy.   _6_

_4_   I am able to risk being myself.

I am really very different from everyone else.   _3_

_7_   I am self-sufficient.

I am very complex, even to myself.   _3_

_7_   Sometimes I cheat a little.

Most people regard me as inconsistent.   _1_

_4_   Sometimes I feel so angry I want to destroy or hurt others.

I prefer extreme disorder to extreme order.   _5_

(Do not compute totals or subtotals until you finish the inventory.)

_124_ **Subtotal for Left Column   Subtotal for Right Column** _99_

6   C&RT

<u>124</u> **Left Subtotal Brought Forward   Right Subtotal Brought Forward** <u>99</u>
37   35

<u>8</u>   I feel certain and secure in my relationships with others.

New situations challenge me more than they frighten me. <u>8</u>

<u>8</u>   I can accept my mistakes.

I am rarely completely understood. <u>4</u>

<u>7</u>   Some people are stupid and uninteresting.

I become bored rapidly. <u>4</u>

<u>6</u>   I have had moments of intense happiness when I felt as though
I was experiencing a kind of ecstasy or bliss.

I do not like being supervised. <u>7</u>

<u>5</u>   Honesty is not always the best policy.

Often I am more persistent than others are. <u>6</u>

<u>2</u>   I can feel comfortable with less than a perfect performance.

My work is my creation. <u>6</u>

<u>161</u> **Left Grand Total   Right Grand Total** <u>134</u>

SCORING

When you have finished assigning numbers to the statements, go back to the first page of the Creatrix Inventory, add the left column, and write that subtotal in the appropriate blank. Repeat the process for the right column. Transfer the subtotals to the top of the next page. Continue the process until you have a grand total for both columns. Then proceed to Part II, Interpreting Orientations.

Scoring and Interpreting
the *C&RT*

Part II. Interpreting Orientations

ABOUT THE C IN C&RT

Creativity may be defined as the ability to produce unconventional ideas. Those ideas may be as mundane as turning eggshells into little faces or as sublime as Athelstan Spilhaus' floating cities in the Atlantic Ocean. They may be as practical as the salt shaker or as absurd as an alphabet with an astronomical number of letters.

When asked "Are you creative?" many people answer in the negative. Some of these negative answers are correct, but most of them are wrong. Unfortunately, people are most often in situations that demand repetition rather than creativity, conformity rather than diversity. If their actions are unconventional, other people may be suspicious of them or view them as unpredictable.

Restrictions on experimenting with new ideas are imposed on most people from early childhood. Children are instructed to keep within the black lines of the coloring book, and doodling is discouraged. Creating fanciful stories is interpreted as lying, and pretending is tolerated only until a child is a certain age—then it becomes embarrassing. Being out of line—the line to the cafeteria, the washroom, the water fountain, or the playground—is considered bad behavior.

Adults on the job are also caught in a variety of binds. Management may want coordination, implementation, and follow-through performed in the same old way, or the amount of creativity desired may be unclear.

Creativity is measured by originality. In fact, about the only criterion for creativity that researchers agree exists is originality. A small percentage of people live in a phantasmagoric world of wildly imaginative ideas; others are at the opposite extreme—out of touch with daydreams. Most people, however, lie between the two extremes.

"Genius" seems to be the only word available to describe the truly creative thinker. The word is used to distinguish an Einstein from a bright quiz-show participant. Unfortunately—because the word is also used to refer to a person with a high I.Q.—people often assume that creativity and intelligence are related. There is little evidence to support that assumption. Many people with only average intelligence have original ideas, and some of the brightest people seldom have original thoughts. Although I.Q. may be an accurate predictor of success in school and on certain types of jobs, it provides no guarantee about a person's ability to make a unique contribution to any field of work. However, just as I.Q. is distributed on a normal curve, so is unconventional thinking. Some people are extremely unconventional, some are extremely conventional, and most lie somewhere in between.

ABOUT THE RT IN C&RT

Creativity in an organization involves risk taking. Management often claims it wants employees to be creative, but usually it does not welcome the associated risks. In order to present new ideas, the creative person must sometimes be the risk taker. Risk taking may mean that a person tenaciously pushes his or her ideas onto someone else—an employer, a colleague, a department—at some risk to the creator's security, career, reputation, or self-esteem.

Although risk taking is not a trait (i.e., it results from a person's fear of failure, fear of rejection, the cost-benefit factors of a situation, etc.), everyone develops an unmistakable risk orientation over the years. That orientation (high, moderate, or low) may change during different periods in the person's life. The organization's response (e.g., supportive, punitive, conservative, or aggressive) will also affect the member's risk-taking orientation.

When people determine their own orientations, they can predict their own responses to different situations. Being aware of their employers' responses will also help employees to predict how the employers will react to specific proposals. This knowledge permits better management of risk for all concerned.

Risk takers also appear on a normal curve. Those who are completely other-directed, taking all their cues from the organization, make up roughly 16 percent. Those who are almost totally inner-directed, taking their cues only from themselves, make up another 16 percent. The other 68 percent fall between the extremes. Most people take cues, to varying degrees, from both the environment and their own convictions, needs, and interests.

WHAT IS YOUR C&RT ORIENTATION?

Measuring the risk-taking orientation and creative sense of individuals in organizations helps to explain why one organization stagnates and dies, another takes excessive risks and lands in bankruptcy, and yet others are moderately to extremely successful.

As the Creatrix suggests, your creativity and risk-taking orientation can be plotted on a matrix. The vertical scale designates the degree to which you are generally a low, moderate, or high risk taker. The horizontal scale designates the degree of your creative abilities. The Creatrix is further divided into eight zones, each representing a creativity/risk-taking orientation. Although there are shades between the orientations—matters of degree—only the eight "pure" orientations will be described here to provide contrast, illustrations, and clarity.

The four orientations in the corners represent people who rank either extremely high or extremely low on creativity or risk taking. When the extreme types become more socialized, Reproducers (low creativity, low risk taking) may become Modifiers; Challengers (low creativity, high risk taking), Practicalizers; Innovators (high creativity, high risk taking), Synthesizers; and Dreamers (high creativity, low risk taking), Planners.

Plotting Your Scores

Take a moment to mark your scores on the C&RT matrix on page 13. To do this, transfer the grand total from the left column of the inventory in Part I to the corresponding point on the vertical scale of the Creatrix. Draw a horizontal line through that point. Then transfer the grand total from the right column of the inventory to the corresponding point on the horizontal scale of the Creatrix. Draw a vertical line through that point. The point of intersection of the two lines will indicate your creativity/risk-taking orientation.

Interpreting Your Scores

The following section presents a detailed view of each orientation. As you study your own orientation, remember that these interpretations are based on only two variables of your personality and behavior. Nevertheless, they provide a window through which to examine yourself while keeping in mind the many other factors that help to make you what you are.

After examining the description of your own creativity and risk-taking orientation, look at the descriptions of the other seven. You and your colleagues may wish to predict one another's orientations. The pages on which you will find each description are as follows:

The Creatrix

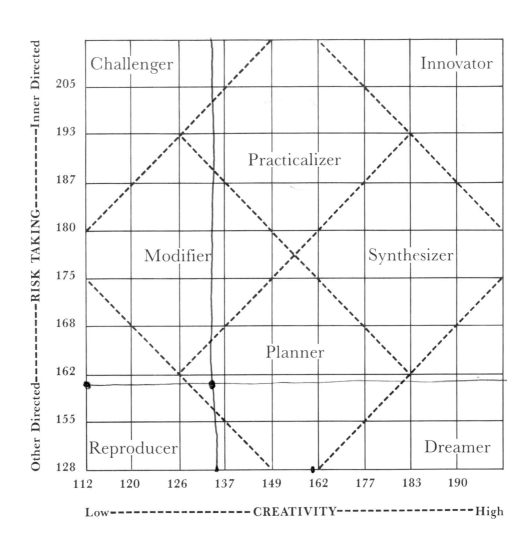

THE REPRODUCER

Reproducers are very responsive to what others think and they seldom use their imagination. Therefore, they rarely entertain unconventional approaches. They seldom see the need for planning, because the past generally holds the best lessons. They usually support control methods, standardization, time studies, industrial engineering methods, quality control, and simplicity of product lines. They resist new systems and techniques, such as computerization and cybernetics, but are anxious to please.

Contributions

As mentioned earlier, most situations demand some repetition. Reproducers are not offended by repetitive tasks—such as filing, stocking shelves, or some phases of accounting—that people with other orientations find boring. They do not care if the task is repetitious as long as they are treated fairly. Reproducers are often the backbone of the organization and provide the control and predictive functions that are necessary for good management. However, despite the fact that many organizations could not exist without them, reproducers often do not receive the appreciation they deserve.

Hindrances

Reproducers sometimes become stuck in ruts. When change occurs, they may continue to perform tasks that no longer need to be done or attempt to use old methods for the new tasks.

THE MODIFIER

Modifiers are somewhat creative and are in the center portion of the normal curve of risk taking. They take what is and add to it. Modifiers rarely discover a new use for an old item, but they may move two machines closer together so that one person can operate both at the same time. They are likely to add paragraphs to a manuscript or to paint furniture a color that shows less dirt. Because of an apparent need to be liked or to go along with the desires of others, and because their proposed alterations are rarely threatening to others, Modifiers are usually valued by their organizations.

Contributions

Modifiers can usually be counted on for the constant little improvements so necessary for lowering the costs of production, marketing, and management. They may suggest turning a form crosswise for easier use, changing the shape of a mold, or using a different type of material. Although not exceptionally creative, Modifiers take moderate risks and install what they want—then tell someone. However, they are willing to return to the old way if management so desires. They are most likely to provide safe, incremental improvements.

Hindrances

Perhaps the greatest weakness of Modifiers is that they can never be counted on for the brilliant solution. Neither can they be counted on to fight very hard for their own suggestions.

THE CHALLENGER

Challengers are consistent risk takers with few new ideas. They become discontent when change is slow. Sometimes they appear to be nihilists or, at least, to want change for its own sake. In a group situation, the Challenger is the person who presents an excellent analysis of why something will not work. A Challenger is frequently told, "Don't criticize this idea unless you have a better one" and is generally not the most popular member of the organization. Challengers rarely have better ideas, but those offered by other people seldom appeal to them. The Challenger's energy lies in wait for the really creative idea by the person (the Dreamer) who has an aversion to risk taking. Like the Reproducer, the Challenger lacks original ideas; but, like the Innovator, he or she is self-motivated and self-directed.

Contributions

Challengers can serve the organization in any area in which ineffective, inefficient, or improper methods or processes are being used. Sometimes an important contribution is to expose sacred cows. For example, management may create a climate in which certain practices are not discussed; or a middle manager with years of service may have to give up his parking space for the new vice president; or certain important clients may be assigned to the manager's inexperienced daughter, who thereby becomes an instant success. The Challenger will ask openly, "What the hell's going on?"

Hindrances

Because Challengers believe in "telling it like it is," they may destroy where destruction is not needed. For example, a nearly retired, muddling manager may be forced to quit six months early—thus losing his retirement—because a Challenger raised so many questions. Tolerated a little longer, the manager could have left with self-esteem and a good retirement. Also the other employees would have been left with a feeling that each person mattered. Any program that needs time to prove itself may not receive the chance if the Challenger is allowed on board.

THE PRACTICALIZER

Practicalizers are high on risk taking and moderately creative. Although they are no more creative than the Planner, they make ideas work because they will take more risks. A socialized Challenger tends to practicalize new approaches. Practicalizers are often perceived as effective managers. They like taking ideas and driving them through the bureaucratic walls of the organization. Because they are moderately creative, they can recognize the gifts of the Innovator (who tends to be socially less acceptable) and of the Synthesizer, Dreamer, and Planner (who are preoccupied with the product rather than its implementation). Practicalizers are confident that they will be able to convince top management of the need to make major changes. They are bottom-line oriented.

Contributions

Practicalizers are action-oriented and they accomplish things. Often they are the only middle managers who can get a change accepted. They will take the risks, up to a point, because they are confident of their ability to produce. President Johnson said, "Politics is the art of the possible," and Practicalizers are the organization's politicians. They are rarely confused between the right thing to do creatively and what can be implemented. They will always compromise for the possible.

Hindrances

Perhaps the major weakness of true Practicalizers is that they will sell out the super-creative person in the crunch and thus sometimes miss the big payoff. Practicalizers rarely play the long shot. They trade tomorrow's first draft choice for today's winner. By doing so, they risk losing the superstar that a draft choice could have brought.

THE INNOVATOR

Innovators are very high on both risk taking and creativity. They always have a new idea and are often willing to give up their jobs if they cannot obtain the organization's support. To others the Innovator seems just like the Challenger: outspoken, hard to influence, and of a single mind. Unlike the Challenger, however, the Innovator always has a better mousetrap. Innovators are full of alternatives, and any one of these may be better than anything the organization is currently using. Start-up costs for the ideas may be prohibitive, but the Innovator rarely accepts that excuse.

Innovators can sense breakthrough products, which must be accepted from time to time if an organization is to compete. Initially breakthroughs are unpopular, because they involve new technology and various kinds of changes. Innovators are aware of this fact and will fight fiercely for the breakthrough's acceptance. Although usually admired and probably feared, Innovators are viewed as radicals and are rarely at the head of the most-liked list. Innovators continue to believe in their ideas when no one else does. When their ideas are not accepted in an organization, Innovators frequently look for capital to start their own companies.

Contributions

Most major nonincremental successes in American industry are the result of Innovators. (Henry Ford is perhaps the most commonly used example of a man with an idea.) They are not afraid to take risks. In fact, from most people's point of view, Innovators will risk more than they can afford to lose.

Hindrances

Innovators may become so fixed on an idea that they are not willing to wait until the time is right. Innovators feel so strongly about certain potential breakthroughs that they cannot see the implementation problems. When what they want is not forthcoming, they may develop a paranoid idea that the organization is against them or that plots are made in executive suites to block them. Sometimes, of course, these suspicions are true.

THE SYNTHESIZER

Synthesizers are quite creative and generally moderate in taking risks. They are idea- and quality-oriented people. They practicalize conceptually what others think. They take unlikely combinations of people, programs, or products and devise a new entity. Their talents are in taking other people's ideas, adding some of their own, and then making those ideas fit into existing situations. Their ideas will never be as practical or as easily implemented as those of the Practicalizer, but they will develop high-quality ideas that are just short of a breakthrough.

Like the Modifiers, Synthesizers like moderate risks. They believe that the ideas will carry their own weight to produce change. This position makes them appear to be Dreamers or Planners to those who do not understand how far Synthesizers will go to sell their ideas. Synthesizers are usually liked but not always understood. They are socialized Innovators.

Contributions

Synthesizers are often the most highly valued of creative people. They put the good of the organization first and their creativity second. Their moderate risk taking makes them controllable, unlike the Innovator. They plan and organize and often function as peacemakers between warring factions. They see combinations of functions, processes, and people that others do not see. New organization charts or production flows challenge their ingenuity. Good synthesizing managers continually combine the needs of the customer with the organization's talents and resources.

Hindrances

The major blind spot of the Synthesizer is an inability to risk all for a breakthrough. They believe in incremental breakthroughs. They are not supersonic-transport lovers; they want a better jet for their customers now, not later. This so-called weakness is, of course, not a weakness in the organization that also has an Innovator. If there is no Innovator, then the Synthesizer's new ideas, always appealing and usually marketable, will prevail.

THE DREAMER

The most underutilized managers are the Dreamers. They are in the upper 16 percent in creativity and the lower 16 percent in risk taking. Their heads are full of unusual ideas; but because of their lack of aggressiveness, their ideas may look like crackpot schemes to the more conventional. Dreamers fit well in jobs that require planning, demand little risk taking, and provide time to think. They always have a better idea but rarely suggest it unless asked for it. Dreamers are discontent in a company that they know could grow faster by using their ideas, but they are afraid to open up and try to convince the company that their approaches are better. At home the Dreamers may be inventors, tinkers, or TV night owls.

Contributions

Dreamers are most beneficial to an organization when their supervisors are Practicalizers. Since the talents of Dreamers can be described as unmined gold, some other force is needed to implement the original ideas. Dreamers may adequately fill Reproducer niches, but this would be a gross underuse of talent.

Hindrances

The major weakness is obvious: Dreamers are underachievers. Being so other-directed and conforming, they may set regressive patterns that make the risk-taking orientations of the organization's Challengers, Practicalizers, and Innovators even more risky. A company that is too heavily loaded with bright, creative Dreamers is headed for a business disaster.

THE PLANNER

Planners tend to be other-directed. Although not as creative as the Dreamers or Synthesizers, Planners think of ways in which creative ideas might be utilized. Like the Practicalizers, the Planners want creative ideas to be operable, but they do not have the necessary risk-taking capacity. The result is that Planners can make the plans but cannot force them through the channels. Usually they are not feared and are respected for their contributions. They often fit well in a planning department, an architechtural firm, a consulting firm, or a teaching position.

Contributions

Planners often develop alternatives for an organization. They have the ability to write corporate road maps and to design management and operational systems. Planners make good staff people and provide appropriate caution. They may have unusual coordinating abilities that make them capable program managers.

Hindrances

Planners are not doers and will generally avoid taking risks. Even though they are more creative than Modifiers, they will rarely take the risks that Modifiers take, even though they are sold on an idea.

CAN YOU CHANGE YOUR ORIENTATION?

To a certain extent you can alter your environment to meet your own needs and ideals. For example, you could take a different job or pursue a different career. Also, to some degree, you are able to change yourself and your orientation. Although you are a product of your genetic and social origins, you can make certain choices. Some people may want to enter individual or group psychotherapy. Others may engage in training aimed at attitude change, not just how-to-do-it-better techniques. A religious pursuit may help a person to reach a new self-awareness. All of these involvements help people to rethink who they are and where they are going.

You may like yourself just the way you are, and you may be happy with the description of your creativity and risk-taking orientation. You may see yourself as valuable and may not wish to cope with the trauma that generally accompanies personal adjustments. Each orientation contributes something, and you may already be making contributions that you and your organization value.

To apply the concepts of the Creatrix to your own situation and to gain personal benefits from the Creatrix Inventory, consider the following questions. Answer them as honestly as you can.

1. Are your scores indicative of what you really think your orientation is? *yes*
2. Which orientation would you prefer to have? Why? *Practitioner*
3. Which two orientations are most complementary to each other? Why?
4. Which two orientations are most antagonistic toward each other? Why?
5. Would it ever be better for people of similar orientations (a) to be clustered together? (b) to be <u>mixed</u> with people of different orientations? Explain.
6. In what ways can people with different creativity/risk-taking orientations complement each other?
7. Which important creativity/risk-taking orientation is most lacking in your organization? *Challenger*
8. Why are people with that orientation rare or nonexistent in your organization?
9. Could something be done to improve the climate for that orientation? If so, what?
10. Think of six principle types of positions in your organization. What would be the ideal creativity/risk-taking orientation for a person in each of these types of jobs?
11. What problems would occur in the interaction among people occupying those positions if each possessed the orientation that you assigned in question 10?
12. What would you—or could you—do to alleviate the problems of question 11?

Challenger × reprove
Innovator × Dreamer
Opposite ext

BACKGROUND ON THE INVENTORY

Norms: The norms for the C&RT instrument were originally developed from a sample of over 500 employees representing seven organizations. Recently, these original norms were retested. The current norms are based on a population of nearly 200 employees from seven organizations, including three manufacturing firms, one consulting firm, and one architectural firm. Thirty-eight percent of the respondents were female, 61 percent were male, and 1 percent did not state gender. Twenty-three percent of the sample represented middle or top management, 43 percent were in technical support (engineering, research, and development), 18 percent were from salaried support (human resources, marketing/business development), and 7 percent were hourly support (secretary, clerk). Based on the results of the retest, the creativity scales have been adjusted to reflect the new normative data.

General Considerations: An implicit assumption of this instrument is that over a lifetime people develop a general predisposition toward creativity and risk taking. Having no evidence to the contrary, these scales have been constructed with the assumption that individuals will take it when things are "going well" for them. Although it is possible for a recent traumatic incidence in a respondent's life to impact the way he or she scores, the norms given here have been judged as an accurate rule of thumb for interpretive purposes.

Face-validity measures indicate that the results are consistent with what researchers tell us are typical of individuals' behaviors in organizations. New organizational members tend to be greater risk takers than those who have been in organizations for more years. The salaried support staff made up of human-resource, business-development, and marketing professionals scored the highest on risk taking, with top management scoring the lowest on risk taking. After age fifty-five, risk-taking scores decreased in this sample. Newcomers to the organization scored highest on risk taking, with a large drop in these scores for organizational members who had been in the firm for over five years. As was verified in the initial norms assessment, women tended to score higher on risk taking than did men.

Creativity measures suggest that creativity decreases in the first year a person is in an organization. Hourly support, secretaries, and hourly administrative personnel scored much lower on creativity than did any other group. Creativity was highest in people 26 to 35 years of age, and men scored somewhat higher on creativity than did women.

Reliability: One advantage of the C&RT instrument is that it is a self-scoring instrument. However, it is also fairly easy to determine the "right" answer, and the scores are thus prone to exaggeration. This factor creates reliability problems. Nevertheless, users indicate that they tend to use the C&RT as a self-exploratory activity and rarely share their results with others. Reliability is increased in this instrument when it is used that way.

The Creatrix provides nine rows for risk-taking scores and nine columns for creativity scores. However, these rows and columns do not represent equal intervals of scores. For example, the column between scores 112 and 120 represents an interval of eight points, whereas the column between 149 and 162 represents thirteen points. Therefore, the rows or columns that contain fewer points discriminate less reliably when the scores are close to the next row or column. Individuals who find themselves close to another category on the Creatrix may wish to read about the nearest type as well as the type they fit.

Validity: In assessing the validity of this instrument, it is important to consider its intention. The C&RT instrument is not designed to be a test, even though it is in test format. No attempt was made to avoid the "halo effect" in the construction of the instrument and, consequently, if it were a test, it might be possible for respondents to determine the "right" answer. The C&RT was designed for self-assessment and educational purposes. Since the practitioners we have interviewed have confirmed this as a purpose, we have no reason to doubt its validity if respondents using it answer honestly—which they should in an educational/self-assessment situation.

As an educational instrument, users have reported a new or greater understanding of the following:

- The underlying determinants of creativity and risk taking.
- Themselves and their own career needs.
- People for whom they have worked.
- How to deal effectively with individuals whose orientations are different from their own.
- The satisfaction or dissatisfaction they have had in their own careers.
- How to effectively manage a diversified group in order to best utilize their talents.

Descriptive Statistics: In the reassessment, frequency analyses were conducted on all demographic and score data. Table 1 and Figures 1 and 2 give the results of these computer analyses. Breakdowns were also conducted on these frequencies so that the creativity and risk-taking scores could be considered within the contexts of the demographics.

Inferential Statistics: A one-way analysis of variance was conducted on the high, medium, and low scores on each of the risk-taking scales. Results indicated a significant difference (alpha = .00) between these scores. Upon visual analysis of the creativity scores, the researcher decided that a one-way analysis of variance would be contraindicated and thus conducted a one-way analysis of variance on the proposed creativity scale. The results indicated a significant variance between high, medium, and low scores of the scales (alpha = .00).

Limitations: The results of the sample are generalized primarily to organizations that have a demographic make-up similar to that of the sample. Although the type of organization varied in the sample, there was no significant difference between organizations, suggesting that the impact of organization type is minimal. However, variations from the demographics implied in this sample need to be considered by users as they apply the norms.

As previously mentioned, users of this instrument have commented that it is used primarily as a self-assessment instrument. To that extent, the individual results are not usually shared with others. For the most part, the subjects in this study knew that the results would be shared with the researchers. This knowledge might have impacted responses. However, confidentiality and anonymity were guaranteed to subjects to minimize this potential limitation.

Table 1. Overall Sample Demographics and Mean Scores

	Percent of Respondents	Mean Score	
		Risk Taking	Creativity
Gender			
Female	38.1	175	150
Male	60.8	170	155
Years in Organization			
Less than one	8.6	184	157
One to five	32.4	177	153
Five to ten	22.7	170	152
Ten to twenty	22.7	167	154
Over twenty	6.8	169	154
Missing	7.4		
Position			
Top management	7.4	160	158
Middle management	15.3	172	156
Technical support	43.8	171	152
Salaried support	18.2	180	161
Hourly support	6.8	162	139
Missing	8.5		
Age			
18-25	15.3	174	154
26-35	35.8	175	163
36-45	27.8	169	152
46-55	13.6	173	157
56-65	1.7	163	147
Over 65	.6	156	Missing
Missing	5.1		
Overall Mean		172	153

N = 176

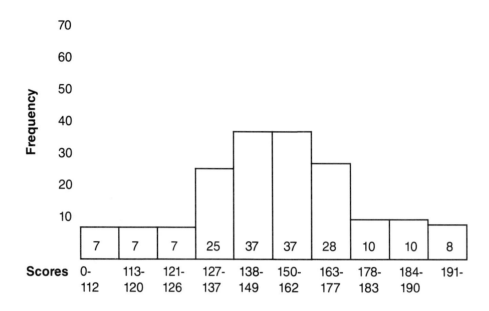

Figure 1. Frequency of Creativity Scores
(Based on New Sample)

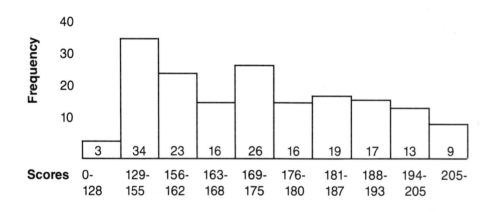

Figure 2. Frequency of Risk-Taking Scores

SELECTED BIBLIOGRAPHY

Becker, H. (1963). *Outsiders.* New York: Free Press of Glencoe.

Brunner, J. (1960). *The process of education.* Cambridge, MA: Harvard University Press.

Byrd, R.E. (1966, October). Training clergy for creative risk taking: A preliminary evaluation. Paper presented at the annual meeting of the Society for the Scientific Study of Religion.

Byrd, R.E. (1968). *Creative risk taking training laboratory: Book of basic readings* (2nd ed.). Minneapolis, MN: Richard E. Byrd.

Byrd, R.E. (1968, November). Redressing the balance with creative risk taking training. *Adult Leadership.*

Byrd, R.E. (1970). Learning stances for creative risk taking. In *Basic reader in human relations training* (Part II). New York: Executive Council of the Episcopal Church.

Byrd, R.E. (1970). Risk taking and encounter. In *Basic reader in human relations training* (Part II). New York: Executive Council of the Episcopal Church.

Byrd, R.E. (1970). *Self actualization through creative risk taking: A new laboratory model.* Unpublished doctoral dissertation, New York University.

Byrd, R.E. (1971, May). How much risk can you afford to take? *Management Review.*

Byrd, R.E. (1973). Creative risk taking: A new tool for human resources development. In T.H. Patten (Ed.), *OD-emergent dimensions and concepts.* Alexandria, VA: ASTD.

Byrd, R.E. (1973). Self actualization through creative risk taking. In D.W. Johnson (Ed.), *Contemporary social psychology.* New York: J.B. Lippincott.

Byrd, R.E. (1975, June). Daring to be different. *Industry Week.* Also in L.J. Loudenback (Ed.). (1976). *Student manual of practical marketing.* Santa Monica, CA: Goodyear.

Byrd, R.E. (1977-1981). C&RT books I and II. In *3M career development workbook.* St. Paul, MN: 3M Company.

Byrd, R.E. (1978). *A guide to personal risk taking.* New York: AMACOM. Also translated into Finnish. (1982). Helsinki, Finland: Oy Rastor A.D.

Byrd, R.E. (1982). *A guide to personal risk taking* (cassette recording). New York: AMACOM.

Byrd, R.E. (1982). *Managing risks in changing times.* Basking Ridge, NJ: American Telephone & Telegraph.

Byrd, R.E. (Ed.). (1984). *Managing risks in changing times.* [Multimedia course]. Minneapolis, MN: Concourse.

Edwards, B. (1979). Drawing on the right side of the brain. Los Angeles, CA: J.P. Tarcher.

Gibb, J. (1978). *Trust.* Los Angeles, CA: Guild of Tutors.

Herbert, F. (1976). *The dune trilogy.* New York: Berkeley.

Keyes, R. (1985). *Chancing It.* Boston, MA: Little, Brown.

Kogan, N., & Wallach, M.A. (1964). *Risk taking: A study in cognition and personality.* Westport, CT: Greenwood.

McClelland, D.C. (1976). *The achieving society.* New York: Irvington.

Pinchot, G., III. (1985) *Entrepreneuring.* New York: Harper & Row.

Reisman, D. (1950). *The lonely crowd.* New York: Doubleday.

Taylor, C.W. (1964). *Creativity, progress and potential.* New York: McGraw-Hill.

Tillich, P. (1957). *Dynamics of faith.* New York: Harper Brothers.

Viscott, D. (1977). *Risking.* New York: Simon & Schuster.